Be Your Own
SANTA CLAUS

Be Your Own SANTA CLAUS

Sandra Gordon Stoltz

First published by Hazelden, October, 1985.

ISBN: 0-89486-341-X

Printed in the United States of America.

This book is dedicated
with
love and appreciation
to
Uncy,
who shared love and knowledge,
and
modeled how to care about folks
and
their emotional and physical well-being.

Buckets of strokes and thanks to . . .

My clients and students, whose stories are told herein, and whose needs gave birth to the BE YOUR OWN SANTA CLAUS workshops, and to this book.

My husband, Gary, and children, Paul and Binnie, who stood behind me when I needed their support. I especially appreciate their understanding and patience in the face of my temporary abdication as wife and mother.

My colleagues and friends, whose love, encouragement, and words of wisdom are part of the manuscript, and are basic to the philosophy I live and teach.

Jean Clarke, for her caring confrontation in spite of my *yes, buts,* and for modeling how to do it.

Karen West, Deane Gradous, Jean Clarke, Sheila Hartmann, and Ann King for editorial assistance and moral support.

Marnie Lilja and Karen West who devoted their creative talents, their enthusiasm, and their commitment to OUR book!

FOREWORD

I love holidays; I always have. But, somehow, some holiday seasons have been more fun and rich and meaningful than others. Sandra Stoltz's book not only helped me sort through what is important for me to provide for myself and others during the entire holiday experience, but, in addition, the book offers sensible, down-to-earth methods and examples of ways I can create a holiday that is what I want it to be.

When I first read the manuscript, I thought Sandra had written this book just for me. However, when I showed it to a friend who hates Christmas, he thought Sandra had written it to help him.

Whatever your attitudes toward holidays, this book is a loving package that can help you make your celebration dreams come true. I invite you to open the package and take the gifts that are in it for you.

Jean Illsley Clarke

PREFACE

As a counselor in private practice, I lead personal growth, Foodaholics, and psychotherapy groups. Every year, around Thanksgiving time, a noticeable change occurs in each group.

I was surprised to discover that people with diverse problems have some common needs during the holidays. Whether they are surrounded by family or alone, whether they feel overwhelmed or underwhelmed, the group members have needed to question, to take stock, to decide what's important to them, and then make some changes in their celebration. Dealing with such issues in the groups helped these people have the kind of holiday that fit for them — that met their needs.

For a number of years, I have facilitated people's changing and learning the coping skills necessary for dealing with the holidays. In order to offer the same opportunities to people who are not members of my groups, I designed a workshop. I call it BE YOUR OWN SANTA CLAUS. Participants found it useful, and have continued to keep me posted on some of the results. Their stories, and the exercises and skills contained in the workshop are part of this book.

I wrote this book in the hope that it would be helpful to more people who are questioning, assessing, and wanting to change some facets of their holiday season and their life.

Here's to . . .

the kind of holiday you want,
the kind of year you want,
the kind of life you want.

CONTENTS

PART I
Introduction

ONE

WHO NEEDS SANTA CLAUS?

Santa Claus is a merry old gent who is loving and caring, thoughtful and giving. He must have a special kind of magic. How else could he know what I want? And how else could he travel so far in just one night?

This jolly being has other marvelous qualities too. He is both exciting and mysterious. He loves doing his job of showering gifts on children everywhere. And sometimes I picture him as not only dispensing tangible goodies, but love and good cheer as well.

There is a fascination, an infinite appeal, in the Santa Claus myth, not only for children, but also for the childlike wistfulness in grown-ups like me. I'll let you in on a little secret. Even though I consider myself an intelligent, sensible adult, I sometimes wait and hope for the fairy-tale magic — for someone who has that special brand of caring, of "psyching out" my needs and meeting them. Do you do that too? I think maybe we're especially prone to do that during holiday seasons.

I have some bad news and some good news. The bad news is that I have wasted a lot of time waiting for Santa Claus-like magic, and then I've been disappointed when no one manages to read my mind accurately or when I end up not getting what I hoped for and expected. The good news is that I haven't had to banish old Santa from my kingdom forever. I've only needed to practice playing his role for myself. I've discovered that I could use him, and all that he represents, in my own behalf, as well as in behalf of others.

You, too, have the ability to be your own Santa Claus, to decide what you want and need from the holiday season, and then take steps to get that for yourself. *Instead of waiting for a mythical being to bring you a joyous holiday, you can don*

3

Santa's red stocking cap and put the magic of the season into your own life.

If your holiday season is basically good, and yet you need to make some changes, you can do that. Or, if you secretly feel sad, lonely, or angry when you think you should be merry, there are some things you can do for yourself. Or, if you feel totally "Bah, humbug!" about the whole thing, and aren't quite content with that, you, too, could choose to use old Santa. I have faith in you. I know if you want to, you have the ability to put the spirit of Santa Claus into your holiday celebration.

People's holiday styles vary greatly. There are those who take an anticommercial stance and believe in emphasizing thoughtfulness, simplicity, and homemade gifts. Others find that course of action sheer drudgery, and welcome the opportunity to buy the goods and services available to them. Some make the holidays a meaningful religious experience, while others feel even more antireligious than usual. Some experience the holidays as being overwhelming, and others feel underwhelmed and lonely.

If you yearn to be more like those special folks who happily, and by choice, pour themselves into holiday preparations, it is possible to find ideas here that fit for you. I'm sharing the stories and suggestions in the following chapters in the hope they will inspire you, both to take action to make your holiday season full of joy and meaning, and also to take better care of yourself. In fact, it is my wish you will also adopt this way of thinking all year long. Give rein to that beautiful imagination you have, trust your feelings, and use your awareness to supply the connection between taking charge of your holiday preparations and celebrations and taking charge of your life!

To sharpen your skills in that direction, I offer you a smorgasbord of ideas and approaches. You can select the options which fit you.

I have approached a smorgasbord in different ways over the years. Do you know which style is yours?

* I have gobbled down everything in sight, and then felt sick.
* I have tasted each item, and then taken second helpings of the foods I really like.
* I have played it safe and selected only the foods I knew I liked.
* I have refused to eat because there was one food I hated.
* I have refused to eat because I did not feel hungry.

The smorgasbord on the following pages will have some ideas you agree with and some you will choose not to use. I hope you will select the offerings that work for you and build a more joyous holiday from them. I invite you to explore the alternatives, to pick and choose, and to arrive at a set of behaviors that are uniquely yours.

TWO

BEING GOOD TO YOURSELF

You can bring your holidays into sharper focus and closer to your ideal by making choices and translating those choices into actions. These choices and new behaviors are the gifts that you can give to yourself. They are the ways in which you can be good to yourself as well as to others during the holiday season. They are the ways in which you can be your own Santa Claus.

In this new and interesting role, you can begin by wrapping yourself a present. It's your *gift box* — a container into which you can put gifts or symbols of gifts that you give yourself.

Choose a box of a size and shape that appeals to you. The only requirements are that it have an easily removable cover and that you wrap it so you can open it repeatedly. Now decorate it with bright paper, paint, ribbon, or whatever other materials and trimmings you want to use. Be playful and creative!

Open your gift box frequently to put in goodies and to sift through and enjoy the goodies already there. Keep opening it to add items right up until the last days of the holiday season, and then through the year, and next year, and the next. By steadily adding new gifts, and taking out those that no longer interest you, you can keep your gift box up-to-date and enticing.

When your box is just the way you want it, you can continue being your own Santa Claus by collecting and savoring the treasures currently available to you. Use big or little sheets of paper, colored 3x5 cards, the back of gift wrapping paper, used greeting cards, tags, or any other supplies that interest you, and you can add to your collection by:
   * writing the words people say to you or about you that
     you especially like.

* writing the words and thoughts you tell yourself that help you feel joyful or powerful — and say more of them!
* writing your positive ideas and insights about the holidays and including those you hear from others.
* adding any words, pictures, or poetry that are appealing to you.
* collecting new snapshots of people you like, as well as special cards you receive.
* buying some special cards, sayings, or posters for yourself. Also adding any other objects you purchase as holiday gifts to you. They could be inexpensive little items that tickle your fancy, or enticing things you encounter while shopping for others.

Keep your gift box handy. Don't stash it away. Keep it visible as a reminder to *be good to yourself*.

One of the best ways to do this is to get strokes. It's probably one of the easiest and quickest too. Strokes consist of, as Eric Berne has written, "any act implying recognition of another's presence," and are, as he says, "the fundamental unit of social action."

Being your own Santa Claus strokes are the actions, words, and evidences that you are recognized as a worthwhile person. They are both the goodies you collect from others, and the goodies you give yourself. Both are valuable.

You can see, hear, feel, smell, or think your strokes. They can be tangible or not. You have the ability to keep the ones that are less concrete from floating away from you. You can add your intangible strokes to your collection and enrich your gift box and your life by describing them on scraps of wrapping paper. Or you can keep a daily log of the goodies you get and give to yourself.

Among the different kinds of strokes are:
Verbal
* I've missed you. Where have you been?
* Hi! How are you?

* I like you.
* You're neat.
* You did a nice job on that.
* You're dynamite!
* You are a good thinker!
* You are a creative problem solver!
* You are lovable and capable!

Physical strokes and touching strokes
(from others)
* putting a hand on your shoulder
* hug
* kiss
* holding hands
* pat on the head
* neck rub
* massage
(to yourself)
* any form of enjoyable exercise
* manicure, shave, or shampoo
* listening to music
* taking a long, luxurious shower or bubble bath
* buying yourself a gadget, a book, or a toy

Written strokes
* mail
* cards
* notes
* written compliments

Telephone strokes
* making contact with people
* hearing a friendly voice
* calling someone who likes you

Is being good to yourself a new idea to you? It was for me not very long ago. Since I see myself as a warm, caring person, I've tried to be good to a bunch of people: my husband, my children, my parents, my husband's mother, other relatives, my friends, neighbors, fellow committee members, co-workers, and boss. They're neat people; I still want to be good to them. The difference is that now I take care of me too! Sometimes I'm even good to me *first!* Some people call that selfishness.

What does the word *selfish* mean to you? The dictionary defines it as "neglecting the welfare of others." *Selfless* is the opposite: "without regard for oneself or one's own interest."

Selflessness has been described as a glorious virtue. Martyrdom and self-sacrifice are its handmaidens. Certainly service to humanity is a strong theme in the Judeo-Christian ethic. There are still clergy who warn against the perils of "me-ism."

But more and more, religious leaders are preaching and counseling the mental health principle of self-responsibility, or meeting one's own needs. They emphasize that the Bible exhorts us to "Love thy neighbor as thyself." One of my clergy friends shared his fear that people, in an effort to live up to that, have taken care of their *neighbors* first and last. He is concerned they have forgotten *thyself* and believes the giving of self to others needs a firm underpinning of self-esteem and self-love. Some additional interpretations might be:

* You cannot love others until you have learned to love yourself.
* You cannot accept others until you have learned to accept yourself.
* You cannot give to others until you have learned to give to yourself.

I was able to love and give to others without learning to love and give to myself. At least I *thought* I was able. However, I've discovered that the *quality* of my loving and giving improves as I learn to be loving and giving to me too. And I realize now that I never really accepted other folks until I started accepting myself.

In order to learn to be good to myself, I had to deal with the battle going on in my head. The forces of selfishness waged against those of selflessness. Then I decided this was a battle in which someone always had to win and someone had to lose. If I'm selfish, others get left out; they don't count. If I'm selfless, I'm not counting myself. Maybe those other folks who are supposed to be selfless toward me aren't doing it. Maybe they're busy, sick, not here, or not willing. In that case I feel left out. I start thinking I don't count with any-body — not with myself, not with others. I think that's what encouraged me to give up being selfless. I needed to be able to rely on at least one person — me!

I prefer to stay off the battleground. I like the idea of *self-fullness*, a concept I first heard used by Judy Wright of the Adler Institute in Minneapolis. *Self-full* means to be full of self, complete, whole, fulfilled. *Self-full* means that I take responsibility for meeting my needs; that I take care of myself, be good to myself, and count myself.

Self-fullness doesn't mean I have to neglect others. If I had an infant, a small child, or disabled parents, I definitely wouldn't want to neglect them. Nor does taking care of them mean that I have to neglect myself. I can figure out some ways to handle the situation so that we both can count. I picture a continuum that looks like this:

1	2	3	4	5	6	7	8	9	10

Self*less*ness	*Self-fullness*	Self*fish*ness
Only Others	We Both	Only I
Count	Count	Count

By becoming a *self-full* person, I am not forced to choose between being a martyr or an inconsiderate boor. Rather, I can choose a middle ground on a continuum, which is to say, "You count, and I count, too." However, I'm finding my own journey toward *self-fullness,* and that of others I've watched, to be an evolutionary process. We've needed to be first on occasion, or for a little while. This is especially true for those of us who have a long history of putting ourselves last, of not counting ourselves at all. Evidently we did not take a selfish position when someone else's welfare was at stake because the important people in our lives have survived intact! We still do slip back at times to our old familiar selfless position, but that happens less and less.

I've learned the gentle art of *selective neglect*. That means I give other folks credit for being able to meet their own needs and for being good problem solvers. I am flexible and make occasional exceptions, such as when others are tired or ill. The following are examples of *selective neglect*.

* Refusing to take over the duties of a co-worker who repeatedly accomplishes little in the morning and then must leave promptly at five P.M.
* Agreeing to tie shoelaces once a week for a five-year-old who says: "I can't," but does know how.
* Expressing regrets instead of dashing out at eight P.M. for a school-aged child who once again has forgotten to tell me about some supplies needed for tomorrow.
* Occasionally handing down the peanut butter jar to a resourceful three-year-old who can concoct a very messy, but highly satisfactory, sandwich for lunch.
* Continuing to eat instead of getting up to refill the glass of a family member who is unoccupied and sitting closer to the refrigerator.

At first I eliminated a few of the ways I took care of others because I needed to do that for me. I was drowning in chores, expectations, obligations. What soon became clear to me as I made changes is that I wasn't the only one who was benefiting — so were the folks I love the most. Choosing to be *selectively neglectful* turned out to be a caring thing for me to do, because their independence, ingenuity, and pride soared! My children, especially, were capable of far more than I gave them credit for. I had actually been stifling their growth, their sense of responsibility and achievement.

Could that also be true for some of the people who are important to you? Suppose you feel and act cheerful and enthusiastic as you go about your holiday preparations because you are being good to yourself; doing more of what you choose to do and less of what you thought you had to do. Here are some more ways in which your becoming a *self-full* person might also be good for others:

* You're probably more fun to be with. You are apt to be better company for all but the most determined grumps or Scrooges.
* Your positive attitude may even be contagious.
* The *quantity* of your giving to others may diminish, yet the *quality* increases.
* And, in that same vein, since you are more likely to be giving because you *want* to instead of because you *have* to or think you *should,* there is a bonus for others — your joy and willingness in the giving.
* And last, but certainly not least, being good to yourself enhances your physical and emotional health and energy. Those who value you will appreciate having you around longer and in better condition.

Are you currently in the business of meeting other people's needs to the exclusion of your own? Have you long put yourself in the position of bottom totem on the pole? If you have placed so little value on your own needs, it may be that those around you have done so also. Possibly you have taught them how to treat you.

Consequently, when you begin to devote more of your thoughts and your energy to pleasing yourself and less to pleasing them, they may not be willing to support you in this endeavor. In fact, they may even do everything in their power to sabotage it! They could try to make you feel guilty. They might compete with you for whose needs take priority. They can probably present a very logical and reasonable case proving the specific need they have is more important than the one you have.

Others aren't *bad* people for using those tactics. They aren't uncaring or nasty. They're just being human. They might be feeling uncomfortable, and probably even scared, about your new and unfamiliar behavior. They are inviting or pushing you back into your old role because that is the familiar and comfortable pattern.

Reverse roles with them for a minute. Imagine you had people who were willing to use their talents, time, and energy in an effort to please you! How would that feel for you? And then, when they started to shift their focus away from you, what would you experience? What would you do? My guess is that you'd hardly be in a position to pat them on the head and say, "My, it's nice that you're taking charge of your life and your needs, and now I have to get better at taking good care of myself."

Do you have the picture? You can understand their need to escalate their old, helpless behaviors, but you can choose to deal with this situation positively. You can pace your changes at a rate that gives them time to adjust also. You can refuse to feel guilty or to fight about it. *No one has the power to make you have guilty feelings, or any other feelings, for that matter. You have to play the compliant victim to let that happen.*

No matter how others decide to behave, you can *still* devote some of your time and energy to you. I hope some of it is prime time, and that you don't just give yourself the dregs. The dregs are when you are so tired or there is so little time left you don't even care about doing what you *want* to do!

Think about what you do or have done in the past to please other people. You probably roll out those little antennae you have in the top of your head, and then you use your sensors to guess what those around you need or want. Often you even have an uncanny ability to know that before they do! Then you decide, and you take action. If at first it doesn't work, you have another go at it. Or, perhaps you experiment with several different ways of pleasing them.

You can, if you choose, use those same methods to please yourself. That lovely intuition of yours, your finely-tuned little sensors, your dogged determination can all be used in your own behalf.

Your antennae may be a bit bent and rusty. You may not have used them for a while, or you may have never experienced using that kind of sensitivity on yourself. Don't let your initial feelings of awkwardness or a few failures deter you. After all, few of your accomplishments were immediate ones. Rather, they grew little by little — they emerged. Think about learning to write, to ride a bicycle, to drive a car. They all took you time, trial and error, and *push*. Sometimes you needed instruction and help from people who already knew how to do the task. And often you enjoyed the support of folks around you while you tried to master this new skill. You may have similar needs while learning to be good to yourself. If so, you can find support and help; I have faith in you. You are an important person. You deserve to have your needs met.

Those of you who live alone could be on the opposite end of the continuum. You may have more than enough time and energy to focus on your own needs, to be Santa Claus to yourself. But are you? Are you taking action to make this holiday season what you want? Or are you waiting and hoping for Santa's magic to come to you or regretting things you cannot change? Experimenting with new behaviors and deeper involvements with other people could help you achieve a fuller sense of self. Use your *self-fullness* to focus on what you need to make the holiday more meaningful, perhaps by discovering and meeting the needs of others. Your rewards could be:

* New friends and acquaintances or deeper relationships with those you already have.
* Growth and new insights from your contacts and experiences.
* Increased energy as a result of the activity and stimulation.

PART II
Taking Inventory

THREE

YOUR HOLIDAY JOB JAR

I offer you a way to find out more about yourself and how you deal with your holidays, a way to help you in making decisions or changes in your preparations and activities.

Picture yourself moving through the holiday season. Start whenever you begin to plan and prepare. If it's Halloween, start then. If you do some gift shopping in July, start then. Use your imagination and your memory to recreate the whole scene for yourself, right up to the festivities themselves.

As you become aware of each task or activity you are involved in during your holiday season, *list* them on the JOB JAR worksheet provided in the appendix. Use pencil to fill it in, so you can erase when you want. Write down a word or phrase to describe each of your holiday activities. You don't have to be perfect — afraid you will leave something out. You probably will! But that's okay, you can add to your list any time. This list is your holiday JOB JAR.

1. Quickly *estimate* how long each task takes. Some of your items may overlap. For example, you may do decorating or shopping while you have house guests.

2. Now *rank* the items on your list according to how important you think they are — #1 = most important. Do this impulsively and quickly, because it merely represents your priorities right now. You can always change your mind. Your emphasis can change a number of times — later today, tomorrow, next week.

3. Review your list. This time, think in terms of tasks or activities you like or want to do, versus those you have to do, or think you should. Mark a **W** next to *want-tos*, or an **S** next to *shoulds*.

4. Next, decide which of the *shoulds* are items you think are important or necessary, and which are other people's

shoulds — tasks they think are important, or expectations you think they have of you. Put an **M** for mine, and an **O** for others.

What feelings have you been aware of as you work on your JOB JAR? As you categorized your tasks? Do you think you have an overwhelming JOB JAR? An underwhelming JOB JAR? Do you feel *shoulded* upon? Or do you feel satisfied, complete, and full of the anticipation of your holiday activities? If it is the latter, perhaps you will want to give this book to a friend, since you may not be interested in exploring new options.

We will revisit the overwhelming and underwhelming JOB JARS in Chapters Six and Seven.

If you think your JOB JAR could stand some improvements, I encourage you to revise it as we go along. For right now, allow yourself the luxury of making another list. Use my WISHFUL JOB JAR worksheet (in the appendix) to create your JOB JAR the way you *wish* it were. Add new activities that would please you. If you have listed tasks you would rather not do, don't put them on your WISHFUL LIST. Or, if they seem unnecessary according to your standards, you may not want to include them.

Now compare your two lists. Ask yourself how you can get them to mesh eventually. Your WISHFUL LIST could be used as your long term goal — your map for shaping holidays of the future. Your ideal holiday may not be entirely possible this year, but you can start working toward your goals. Begin by using your awareness of your wishes to make a few changes.

You can, if you will take action, change the trend over a period of several holidays. Dreams do come true, fantasies come alive for those who are willing to work to make them happen. The first step is to acknowledge your ability to do that.

Life and holidays don't just happen to you, unless you are willing to be helpless and let outside factors or other people take charge of you — your activities, your decisions, your priorities, your time, and your personal space.

Keep your WISHFUL LIST in mind as you go on to the next chapter. We are going exploring into the realm of holiday magic.

FOUR

WHERE'S THE MAGIC?

We're going to take a short trip back into the past. If you have a tape recorder, you could enhance this little journey by recording the instructions. Say them to yourself slowly in a soft, caring voice. You may even want to stop reading right here and let yourself be surprised by what you hear. If so, ask someone to read aloud or record the rest of the instructions.

Whatever method you use, be aware of whether it would feel better for you to be in a quiet corner off by yourself, or whether you want another person nearby. Find yourself a comfortable place to sit or lie down. Find a place in which you feel relaxed and safe. Do whatever you need to feel comfortable. Now close your eyes and breathe deeply. Breathe very deeply and slowly. Feel your breath entering and leaving your body. Feel yourself relaxing more and more each time you inhale, and let your tension go with each breath you exhale. Give yourself a little time to enjoy the silence and to just be with yourself.

Allow yourself in your imagination to once again become the little person you once were. Be three years old, or five, or eight, or whatever age you want. Look around you back then with a child's eyes. See your family, your house, your street, your friends. Notice winter coming on. Notice the hints and signs that the holidays are approaching.

Allow yourself to remember some happy holiday scenes from your childhood. Notice what the people around you are doing. Notice what you are doing. What are you feeling and thinking as you move through these activities? What do you like the most about those scenes? About what do you have the best feelings? What leaves you feeling deeply touched?

Just for the fun of it, create a picture of another holiday season. This one is exactly the way you have always wanted it to be. As you move through your holiday scenes, surround yourself with the kind of people you like. Have them treat you just the way you want to be treated. Allow yourself to experience and enjoy being treated so well. Now picture yourself doing what you most love to do during these special times. Let yourself have fun! Build yourself some happy, exciting scenes. Feel your anticipation, your joy, and the magic of it. Notice what about it is especially magic for you. Notice what means the most to you this holiday season. Slowly move through the scenes, staying as long as you wish.

When you feel satisfied, when you have had enough celebrating, let go of your holiday scenes, and come slowly back into the present. Hang on to your awareness about what was special for you, what was exciting, and where the magic was for you.

I invite you to join me in the belief that our dreams and fantasies are an important part of us, that we have the power to make them come true, at least in part. I wish I could tell you that you can have all your dreams. I regret that isn't always possible. For instance, if sitting on Grandpa's lap is one of my fondest memories and Grandpa is now dead, I am powerless to bring back that particular magic. But maybe I know a kindly soul who is willing to be my foster grandfather. We can recreate some of our childhood magic or our wishful magic by recognizing what events and circumstances are meaningful for us and by acting on that knowledge. We can make the past and our dreams a part of our present celebration.

The first step in acting on these beliefs is a matter of internal housekeeping — the way I think about myself and my life. Life is more joyful when I accept the little girl who still inhabits part of my grown-up body, mind, and emotions. I can include that little person in my holiday season and my life by acknowledging and meeting some of her needs and wants.

I know that no matter how mature and reasonable I am, the childlike part of my personality is with me still. If I inhibit myself and try to be just one kind of person, like a logical and efficient person, or a caretaker, good parent type, I'm keeping myself from becoming all that I can become. I'm denying my total humanity. I'm denying myself the richness, the fullness of my existence. My own experience is that accepting and uncaging that little being has increased my energy and my enjoyment of life.

We don't have to act like grown-ups all the time. And we certainly don't have to think and feel only like grown-ups. Usually, it is the childlike part of us that has fun and loves festivities. And the little boy or girl in us is the one who feels the magic and the meaning of the holidays.

What does the little person in you need? What is your magic? Do you need more magic? If so, what are you going to do to put more meaning and excitement in your holiday season or your life? Decide how you can recreate some of the joys of your ideal holidays. Decide what you will do to increase your magic and fun, or whom you will ask to help you.

Here is how some people added more magic to their celebrations:

Randy discovered that midnight mass was magic for him. He remembered as a little boy how awed he felt by the beauty, the music, and the color of this service. He sadly realized he hadn't gone since his high school days. Everyone he knew now partied during the holiday season. And Christmas Eve was the occasion that topped them all! Randy wasn't too surprised when no one he asked would join him for the service, but he decided he would go. His irreverent friends made great fun of his leaving the party early, and Randy felt uneasy about attending that special service alone for the first time in his life. But he *loved* it! The magic was still there! He did put meaning back into his Christmas.

* * * * * *

25

Corinne remembered how she loved surprises and asked her husband, Archibald, to surprise her this year instead of discussing in advance what was top priority for this year's big gift. He did as she requested, and the surprise he sprang on her was a stereo. Her continued delight is a great source of joy to him. Every time she plays a record, she relives the magic of her holiday surprise!

* * * * * *

Dave and Tammy recalled the fun and excitement of un-stuffing stockings. They felt silly starting again now that they were an adult family. They did it anyway — they stuffed stockings for each other with a combination of grown-up gifts and little kid goodies and jokes. It worked! They had a barrel of fun on Christmas morning! It added the extra spark they wanted to their celebration.

* * * * * *

Are you aware of some new activities that you want for the holidays? If so, add those to your JOB JAR. You may also want to reorder the priorities in your life now. Maybe you want to allow more time for fun and magic. Maybe you know what you need to do to make your holiday more meaningful. If that is what you want, and you've made some decisions, write them down. Present your written plans to yourself as another gift and put them in your GIFT BOX.

If you are still lacking specific ideas, don't quit now. Some of the suggestions or examples in Chapters Six and Seven may better fit your needs or spark your creativity.

FIVE

LEAPFROGGING THE PITFALLS

Life and holidays don't just happen *to* you, unless you are willing to be helpless and let circumstances or other people take charge of you — your activities, your decisions, your priorities, your time, or your personal space. *You are in charge!*

Remember this while we explore some pitfalls. Folks like me stumble into a few of these. Many of these problems are not only holiday hazards, but can occur any time of the year. They are *potential* pitfalls for *some* people *some* of the time. What is a pitfall for me could well be a happy choice for you.

The numbered paragraphs in the rest of this chapter point out problem areas. If I'm behaving in the same way as the people in the examples, and yet it doesn't feel like a problem to me, the chances are that I'm being good to myself in one or more of the following ways:

* I am *choosing* to take on certain tasks or activities.
* I feel good about doing it.
* There are rewards that make it worthwhile for me.
* I am meeting my own goals or behaving according to my own standards.
* I am taking care of my own needs too.

My wish is that you will use the pitfall descriptions for your own awareness. When you begin to feel uneasy, you can recognize the hazards and avoid wallowing in the pits! Instead, you can go leapfrogging over the pitfalls! (Chapters Two and Eight also have some leapfrogging techniques.)

Let's peek in on David. He has a demanding job and he has a family. In order to manage his grandiose Christmas preparations, he begins before Halloween to put in eighteen-hour days. In addition to his existing commitments, he is doing a lot of planning and scurrying around. He really likes scouting out the perfect gifts and wrapping them elaborately. He wants them to be spectacular, so everyone will be thrilled and excited. But before long, he feels rushed and tired.

Instead of having the family time he wants during this special season, he ends up doing some of his tasks very early in the morning or late at night when no one is awake to share them. Besides, he's missing his son's Saturday hockey games in order to fit in all the shopping.

David is also planning a fantastic party for his office staff. He figures it should boost morale considerably. He puts thought, time, and effort into preparing for the party. By the time the big event rolls around, David is too exhausted to enjoy it himself. What a pity! David loves parties, and he did this one just the way he thinks parties ought to be.

1. What David has done is give up his here and now. He is *futuring*. He is not enjoying much of what he is doing in the present because he is hurried and tired. Some people, like David, plan, work, and *suffer* to set up a future event that lasts only a few hours. And feeling emotionally overwhelmed as well as physically exhausted can take the fun out of those very special few hours.

2. David is aiming to create a spectacle or production. I wonder if he believes the formula that *meaningfulness and good feelings are equal to quantity plus perfection*?

3. Could David be *orchestrating the celebrations* for a whole bunch of people? Will he give himself bad reviews when it isn't enjoyable for him? What will happen if others aren't festive enough?

Clarissa is David's wife and she is surrounded by folks who are excited, in high spirits, and eagerly anticipating Christmas. She can't imagine why, but she just can't seem to get into the swing of it. And the worst part is that the more she is with these deliciously happy folks, the more she is convinced something is wrong with her. She thinks maybe she is even getting more blue instead of better.

4. Clarissa is not alone in her belief that *only certain emotions and attitudes are right* at this time of year — emotions such as joy, merriment, and good will. People like Clarissa tend to feel guilty or inadequate when their feelings or attitudes are less than positive, or when they seem *inappropriate.*

5. I know when I deny my feelings, I often become depressed and fatigued. I'm not only taking the energy that is wound up in my emotions and attempting to bottle it up, but I am also using a lot of my energy trying to keep the cap on that bottle.

Getting back to David — he knows Clarissa is vaguely unhappy, and he feels responsible for changing that for her. So he buys a huge flocked tree. He doesn't really like flocked trees, but he knows Clarissa does. He also gets her a new microwave oven for Christmas. He thinks she will be delighted. He can't really afford it and will have to make payments for most of the next year, but making Clarissa happy is definitely worth it.

Much to David's chagrin, Clarissa was picturing a very small and delicate flocked tree. In fact, her fantasy included delicate ornaments too, and the ones they have accumulated are much too large and heavy. David had no way of crawling into his wife's dreams or wishes, and she shared only a small part of them with him.

David found out he was right. Clarissa did adore having a microwave. Strangely enough though, she was not only thrilled with her gift, she was also appalled! She knew they couldn't afford it, and the expense frightened her. David was crushed! He felt inadequate as a human being and as a provider.

6. He took on the responsibility for Clarissa's feelings. He is trying to *"fix" her feelings,* to turn them into the *right* ones. Once again, he is conducting the Christmas orchestra.

7. David tried to guess what would make another person happy and then did whatever was necessary to meet those

needs. He also allowed his self-esteem to become involved. He operated under the belief that *he has to please others in order to be liked or accepted*. Consequently, when he wasn't able to please Clarissa, he felt worthless, inadequate, and unlovable.

8. He also *overextended himself financially*. He might have to curtail spending for some time. Six months from now, when he is feeling strapped for cash, he might be angry, depressed, or scared about that.

* * * * * *

Percy is a widower who spends most of his holiday season reliving his past celebrations. He remembers how disappointed he was as a child. They were so poor, and Mom and Dad weren't very merry during holidays; they were mostly tense and angry. It wasn't much fun for little Percy. Percy also remembers the lovely holidays they had when his own children were young. He deluged his kids with presents to make up for all those he didn't get as a little boy.

9. Percy is *past-ing*. He is diminishing the reality, the aliveness of living in the present. By using his time and energy to dwell in the past, he is neglecting to take charge of the holiday that is here and now. He is helpless to change what happened in the past. He cannot make his boyhood joyful no matter how hard he wishes it. Reliving fond memories makes him warm and happy. Unfortunately, he cannot bring back the good old days when his little house was crowded, noisy, and fun during the holidays. I wonder what he might do about it *this* year? Do you suppose he could find another family that is crowded, noisy, and fun?

* * * * * *

"Holidays equal wall-to-wall togetherness. Togetherness is good stuff. The more, the better," Vanessa thinks. So she chauffeurs the kids, gift shops with them, takes them to the theater and movies, goes to a number of family parties, and gives some herself. Mom comes to stay for two weeks. On the big day, Vanessa has the entire family including aunts, uncles, and cousins for a vast feast that she is determined will out-shine Cousin Annabelle's last year.

Vanessa feels very tense and angry when Mom raves over brother Bob's gift more than hers. Vanessa spent more than she should have, and she is jealous that Bob has so much money to throw around. In fact, Vanessa sees every other sentence coming out of his mouth with a dollar sign in front of it.

Mom consistently criticizes the way Vanessa is doing things. There's nothing very substantial to which Vanessa can reply. Rather it is just a steady "pick, pick, pick." Much of the time, Vanessa is a self-confident, capable woman, but she is beginning to feel more and more like an inadequate, helpless little girl.

Vanessa is setting herself up for failure in three ways:

10. She is *failing to meet her own needs* for quiet, for relaxation, and for withdrawal time.

11. She is *sacrificing herself to the togetherness myth.* Maybe in her particular family, less is better, rather than more.

12. She is *turning holidays into competitive events.* She is vying with others to buy the nicest gifts, throw the most lavish party, or have the most dazzling holiday wardrobe. The satisfactions may be few; she may rarely get to feel as if she has won. She could also be overextending herself both finan-cially and physically.

* * * * * *

Heloise is a nurse. She likes having a quiet holiday, and then going to work for the 3 P.M. shift. Her co-workers think that's just wonderful, because they prefer to have the day off. They have plans that are quite different from Heloise's. But they feel very sorry for her. "Poor Heloise. No big wing-ding!" Heloise is getting tired of explaining why she likes a quiet holiday. She reads in the magazines and hears on the television about all this big deal holiday stuff. Heloise begins to feel left out and starts to carry around a big sack full of self-pity. Then on the holiday, instead of bouncing happily through her duties as she often does, Heloise drags herself through the hospital corridors.

13. Heloise is *allowing the media and others to influence her expectations and activities.* She is buying into the myth that a big production makes a happy holiday, and that other styles of celebrating — or the absence of celebration — are unacceptable. She may even be confusing her aloneness, that quiet intimacy she has previously enjoyed, with loneliness.

* * * * * *

Let's take a look at the way Loretta does things. Loretta gets a big kick out of baking. The house smells so good, and she gets to try intriguing new recipes. She also likes writing letters to faraway friends and acquaintances. With many of them, it is the only contact she has, and she cherishes it.

Loretta's mom thinks elaborate decorations are a must. And then there is a special fruitcake Mom insists is essential. Loretta spends a couple days putting up decorations and a couple baking her mother's fruitcakes.

Loretta's husband, Malcolm, came from a family which always had the neighbors in for a tree trimming party. Loretta would prefer to have a festive night with their own family stringing popcorn and cranberries and all the other fun stuff that goes with tree trimming. But she prepares for the party, and labors to get the food and house ready. She feels devastated when the party gets boisterous and her children flee to their rooms. One of her neighbors even gets drunk. That's not Loretta's idea of tree trimming atmosphere!

Because she took on added tasks of cooking, cleaning, and decorating, Loretta has to scrunch her favorite activities of baking cookies and writing letters into whatever time is left. As it turns out, she has time only for short notes and one new recipe.

14. Loretta is *failing to discriminate among the expectations:* her own, other people's, and those expectations which could be categorized as traditions. By accommodating and striving to meet all those *shoulds,* Loretta is allowing them to become a burden. A heavy load of shoulds is comparable to carrying Santa's 100-pound sack for the whole holiday season. Is it any surprise that people like Loretta end up with resentment, exhaustion, irritability, or depression as their Christmas gifts to themselves?

15. Loretta is also choosing to work hard and *suffer* over her holiday preparations. Working hard is a joyful choice for some folks. Suffering is optional.

* * * * * *

You've had a chance to see how some people let their holiday magic, or fun, or meaning slip away from them. Now you know some of the ways in which folks fail to be good to themselves.

As you revisit your JOB JAR, I hope that recognizing these pitfalls will help you hold on to the parts of your holiday preparations and celebrations you like. Be good to yourself — be your own Santa Claus by adding whatever you need to make it better.

PART III
Planning and Acting

SIX

THE UNDERWHELMING
JOB JAR REVISITED

If your list of tasks and activities lacked the quality and/or quantity you want, this is the time to explore ways of adding to your holiday celebration. If your holiday is hardly a festive one because you are lonely, there are many ways you can arrange to be with people. Age has little to do with it, nor does marital status. Whether you are a single, a senior, or a member of a small nuclear family, you can usually find a way to be with people if you will only take action and ask! You can ask around among your friends, acquaintances, neighbors, and co-workers. Be persistent; it doesn't always work the first time, or the second. Do not confuse refusal with rejection. They are a world apart.

I can already hear you saying a whole string of *yes-buts*. Yes-buts are the excuses you make, either in your head or out loud. They are the obstacles you use to keep yourself from getting what you want:

* Yes, but they won't want me. I'm too old for them.
* Yes, but they won't want me. I'm too young for them.
* Yes, but they're a big, happy family, and I'd be intruding.
* Yes, but they have out-of-town guests.
* Yes, but I'm shy.
* Yes, but I have no transportation.
* Yes, but it costs too much.
* Yes, but it's too forward.
* Yes, but they're too busy.
* Yes, but they might not like me.

Are some of these excuses familiar or do you have your own special ones? There is probably a grain of truth to each one of your objections, or at least the possibility that you might turn out to be right, so you can convince yourself that your situation is hopeless. You cannot, however, convince me. I know there's at least a bit of risk every time I try something new. I also know I'd never do anything different if I sat and worried about it instead of taking some risks. And most of the time my fears turn out to be groundless. Isn't that amazing? Could it be that you have a lot of groundless fears too?

I offer you a different way of approaching obstacles:

POSSIBILITY THINKER'S CREED
By Dr. Robert H. Schuller

When faced with a mountain
I will not quit!
I will keep on striving
Until I climb over,
Find a pass through,
Tunnel underneath. . .
Or simply stay and
Turn the mountain into
a gold mine,
With God's help!

You could even use that to supply yourself with a few more yes-buts. For instance: "Yes, but I don't believe in God." Or, "Yes, but He's not on my side lately." Or, "Yes, but . . . ."

Yes-buts will help you if you want to keep things the way they are. Yes-buts will help you if you want to hang onto feeling forlorn or left out.

Taking the First Steps

I invite you to take some steps to change your situation. I know that new and unfamiliar behaviors can be uncomfortable, awkward, and even scary. But I hope you will take a minute to visualize how rewarding your life would be if you took the risk of changing. Then think back to the risks you have taken in the past that have reaped rewards for you. Do you remember times when the things you feared never materialized, the risk was less than you had expected? Even when it was not, you survived — after all, you are here now reading this book. I know you can not only adjust to change and survive, but you can also have a higher quality of existence in that survival!

Let's get back to the issue of taking risks to become more involved with other people. You can lessen those risks by being assertive and matter-of-fact. When you approach others about including you in their plans, be positive. First tell yourself that you are a worthwhile person who has something to offer others, then act upon that assumption. Resist any temptation to play "poor little me" appealing to their sense of pity as a reason for including you. They may resent you and you may not like yourself much either.

Start off with requests for strokes or for small scale involvement to get your courage up and practice asking. You may want to ask:
* "Will you call me Thursday morning?"
* "I need a hug."
* "Don't you think I did a good job on that?"
* "How about having lunch with me tomorrow?"

Now go on to ask for what you need to make your holiday better. Some of the possibilities are:
* "Shopping together is so much more fun. Are you interested?"
* "Will you join us?"
* "Let's have a party together. What do you think?"
* "I'd love going to church with you. Does that fit into your plans?"
* "We like new people at our celebration. Will you come?"
* "I'm alone this year and would love to join you for your holiday celebration. Will you think about that and let me know?"

* "I'm interested in spending the holiday with your family. Does that interest you too?"
* "Would you be willing to include me in your festivities?"
* "I think of the holidays as a big family occasion, and we have such a small family now. How about our getting together?"
* "Do you know of someone who is looking for a celebration? We want to add guests to our celebration this year."

The above are a few ideas meant to get you thinking about your own specific way of asking. Here's a hint: do not hint! Be sure to include an actual question somewhere in your request, otherwise you are putting your responder in the position of having to supply the missing link. They may disappoint you and fail to do so. Ask for a response too, but not necessarily an immediate one. Although these examples may sound abrupt, they do model good, straight communication. You may be more comfortable softening your request. Asking from a self-full position, you can offer your talents and willingness to contribute to a holiday celebration. You might combine your request to be included with an offer of your help. This honors both the host and you, the guest. Some ways to do that are:
* "I will help you serve and clean up."
* "I will come early and help you set up and do last minute preparations."
* "I will keep the little folks occupied, so you won't be interrupted while you do the preparations."
* "I could babysit while you do some of your gift shopping."
* "I make good pies and will be responsible for the dessert course."
* "I love to cook and would be glad to contribute whatever you least like to make."
* You may prefer to bring wine, candy, fruit, or other delicacies to the gathering.

These options are but a few of those available to you. Being creative, thinking of your own way of asking, and taking credit for what you can offer will yield a number of alternatives if you want to reciprocate or earn your way.

You can choose to believe you are superfluous at any holiday gathering — a fifth wheel. In fact, you may even believe you are a burden. Only you can make that true or untrue. You can choose to be a blessing instead of a burden.

You can be an invaluable asset to any group. You are an asset simply because you are you. Release your uninhibited self, your childlike self, at holiday time. You could have more fun that way, and so will others. You can also be an asset by offering yourself as a willing pair of hands. You have yourself to give as a gift.

Many people would be delighted rather than feel imposed upon when you ask to join their holiday festivities. They would think you care about them and wanted to be with them during this special time.

Large, congenial families are often willing and eager to expand to include an additional person. In fact, they may have a pattern of having done so through the years. It might as well be you this year!

Less congenial families often have a far more enjoyable celebration when outsiders are included. Under those circumstances, they are likely to bring out their company manners and act more cordially to each other. Think of the huge favor you would be doing for the family members simply by being present! Hint: If you belong to such a family and the time of holiday togetherness is not to your liking, take some action in your own behalf. Ask a friend or neighbor to join you. It may not only increase your enjoyment, but also alter the family interactions. Or you could find another group to be with.

Here are two examples of how some folks added to their UNDERWHELMING JOB JAR, became Santa Claus to themselves, and had the kind of celebration they wanted.

Roger and Stephanie Gray are a retired couple who live next door to the Johnsons. The Johnsons have two small children. The Grays arranged a brief Sunday afternoon visit, at which time they shared with the Johnsons the news that their daughter Lucy, a stewardess, would not be in town for the holidays, neither would Roger, Jr., who would be visiting his in-laws. Stephanie said: "I know your folks will be staying here, and we would like to meet them. I think we will have much in common. We would like to celebrate the holiday with you. Roger can show your folks around town, if you like, and I could help with the little ones. How does that strike you?" The Johnsons were enthusiastic. In fact, to them the Grays looked like Stephanie Claus and Roger Claus.

* * * * * *

The Conners have two teenaged children. They asked Lydia Smith, the single parent of a preschool child, to join in their holiday feast. Their mutual friends, the Greenes, heard about this arrangement, and asked to be included. Each family contributed to the preparations, although the Conners insisted on doing a large share of it themselves.

The three small families had expected that their being together would be fun, and it was. It was more interesting and stimulating than each family's usual small gathering, yet it felt cozy and comfortable. The children got along well despite the wide range in ages. They decided to make this an annual event.

* * * * * *

Have you thought of any more ideas about how you can have a better holiday by being more involved with people? You might add to your festive spirit by volunteering at a seniors' residence, a pediatric ward, or a charity dinner. You can help serve a holiday meal, play cards or games, or read to people. You will find yourself welcomed and rewarded. Or, you could play Santa at a store, a church, a party, or a community event. Or, you can deliver holiday baskets to the needy for your church or another social agency.

One small step, one initial change, has a way of snowballing and having a profound effect. Here's an example.

Vernon was a recent widower who decided to spend Christmas Day at a center for the disabled. He helped feed a couple of people, read a story from a new book to a bedridden youngster, and taught a young man named Tad to play cribbage. Tad was a paraplegic as the result of a motorcycle accident. He was obviously depressed. Vern visited frequently. Tad had a quick mind and took great pleasure in subsequently outplaying his teacher. They became cribbage buddies and much more. Upon his release from the center, Tad took an apartment with some friends in Vern's building. The relationship has meant a great deal to both men. Each would have been more lonely without the other.

* * * * * *

There are many ways you can reach out in order to be with people. You can have a party. You can host the holiday feast. If your living quarters are too small, join forces with a friend, neighbor, or co-worker who has more space.

You could say, "I want to cohost a party with you. If you are interested in having it at your place, I will take charge and organize it. I will also do half of the preparation chores and pay half the expenses."

Tracy is an attractive single woman who finds Christmas with her parents so unpleasant that she has preferred to be alone the last few years. That had felt better, but it was still somewhat depressing for her. This year she decided to keep herself busy and have a party. She and a friend gave it together. The guests were each asked to bring a favorite food. It required a fair amount of calling and planning on Tracy's part, but as a result of those efforts, she was invited to another party and scheduled two special evenings out — one at the theater and one at a basketball game.

During the party, Tracy and three of her guests decided to spend Christmas Day together. They were not interested in a traditional celebration, so spent the day nibbling exotic appetizers, playing cards and games, and listening to records. It turned out to be a silly, lighthearted day — the best Christmas Tracy could remember.

* * * * * *

Cassy was formerly a gourmet cook, and she was a fine baker. What she fondly remembers about Christmas season is making hundreds of ornate, varied cookies. She particularly missed the days when she and the children would be merrily chattering at each other while working on countless batches of cookies for friends, neighbors, school, and office. But now she had no one to bake for, and she was feeling very sorry for herself.

Cassy finally became fed up with feeling sad, lonely, and useless. She volunteered her services to the Cub Scouts and Brownies. She held cookie baking sessions at her house, and the youngsters helped her, learned from her, and had fun with her. Each child brought a small sum of money, which paid for the ingredients, and then divided their cookies and took them home. Cassy became known as the "cookie lady," and she was much in demand! In addition, some of the children regularly stop by to chat with her, and she once again keeps the cookie jar full.

* * * * * *

Wayne used to be married. He was worried that the holidays would be pretty awful for him since his children would be away at their grandparents'. He was bothered and unhappy about the whole holiday season. He had to buy a lot of gifts for relatives, and he didn't know where to start because his wife had taken care of that. Wayne was beginning to see why she was always grumbling about the shopping. Wayne talked to his sister who lived in a nearby town, and they decided to divide the gift buying. Wayne elected to handle the selection of all the toys. He felt like a little boy again when he was in the toy stores. It would be wonderful if the children who received those gifts enjoyed them half as much as he did selecting them.

Wayne began to spend a lot of time with his sister and her family. They had some heart-to-heart talks, and began, for the first time, to really feel close to each other. His nieces and nephews loved to play with Uncle Wayne, and that helped him fill the emptiness he felt when his own children weren't around.

* * * * * *

Eula was another woman who liked to fuss with food, particularly during holidays. Sometimes she traveled to visit her kids and grandkids in a distant city, but one year she didn't feel up to that. She knew, though, that she'd have to think of a way to keep herself occupied and spend some of her time with people, or she would feel depressed. She was friendly with the crew at her local grocery store. So she made a luncheon date with them at their convenience. She arranged to bring lunch in for them at a time when the maximum number of people could be available to meet in the back room. She provided the food, and they provided the company, the fun, and the appreciation. They became better friends than ever. Eula also made similar plans for dinner with a neighbor of hers, a shut-in. It felt so good to have people to cook for again!

* * * * * *

I hope now an UNDERWHELMING JOB JAR is something you *once* had. I hope it's getting filled with activities and tasks that are fun and festive for you. And what about your GIFT BOX? Have you been adding to it? Don't forget to include a little note or poster with some of the ideas you've had. And be sure to write down some strokes to yourself for being so smart and figuring out what you can do — more strokes for being adventurous and trying new things.

SEVEN

THE OVERWHELMING
JOB JAR REVISITED

Haul out your JOB JAR from Chapter Four. How do you feel as you read it? Overwhelmed? Resentful? How have you arranged to put yourself in such a pickle? Notice, I said *you* put yourself in that position. It is my conviction that: *We who feel victimized have allowed that to happen, perhaps have even encouraged it. We have in some sense been willing victims, actively participating in our downtrodden state.*

HENRIETTA'S OVERWHELMING JOB JAR

cards	6 hours
out-of-town letters	10 hours
out-of-town gifts (shopping and mailing)	3 days
other gift shopping	10 days
select a tree	1 day
tree trimming party	2 days
decorate house	1 day
clean house very thoroughly	3 days
my office party	6 hours
Horace's office party	4 hours
neighborhood party	6 hours
church party	4 hours
family feast	2 days
wrap gifts	12 hours
grocery shopping	4 hours
get stocking fillers	5 hours
fill stockings	2 hours
bake cookies	2 days

Discovering If You've Been a Willing Victim

* Are you trying to manage the holiday spirit for others?

Are you spoon-feeding them what you think are the proper doses of excitement and joy? Do you work hard to make sure everyone will be happy?

* In your efforts to please people, do you give away too much of your time, energy, or money and end up feeling depleted?
* Are you attempting to carry out multiple traditions — your parents', your in-laws', yours, and your spouse's? Your neighbors'? Your church's?
* Do you get very little help with your agenda? Do you believe people ought to read your mind, know that you need or want help, and just offer it? Do you believe it just isn't the same if you have to ask for it? Or do you think others won't do as good a job as you can? Or you won't ask them because you think they're too busy?
* What are some other ways you set yourself up to be a victim?

Notice particularly the items on your list that relate to others' expectations, or *shoulds*. How much time and energy are you willing to devote to meeting others' expectations? Or do you plan to go ahead and do what is expected of you even if you are unwilling and feel resentful? What will that cost you emotionally and physically?

I experience resentment as working like a pressure cooker. It simmers and stews until it works up a good head of steam, and then it either chatters and puffs or it explodes all over the ceiling. When you do things resentfully, do you stew silently, creating a tense atmosphere? Or do you chatter and puff away, complaining and nagging? Or are you likely to swallow it all until you reach a point where you issue ultimatums or proclamations: "I've had it! Never again."? Instead of staging such scenes, some people explode inwardly by getting a headache, a backache, an ulcer, or a number of other physical complaints. If that sounds like you, I urge you to stop hurting yourself. My hope is that you will find counsel with a

professional who will help you find healthier ways of dealing
with your resentment.

* * * * * *

We sometimes go through some interesting gymnastics with
the expectations we think others have. We can carry these
conflicting expectations by: bending over backwards, juggling,
weight lifting, long-distance running, or walking a tightrope.

Speaking of weight lifting, Delphine felt a whole bunch of
heavy expectations. She heard them in statements made by
her family members, by her in-laws, and in her husband's
descriptions of his childhood celebrations. She made many
assumptions about the size and shape of celebration that was
expected — the formality of it, the type of entertainment, the
quantity and quality of food, gifts, people present, and the
size of the tree. Delphine assumed that the burden of preparation was hers. Although she enjoyed doing most of her
holiday tasks, they seemed weighty on top of her other
commitments.

When Delphine sat down with her family to find out what
they really wanted, what their priorities were, she scaled down
her grandiose assumptions. Her family members did want to
be part of the planning and the doing. They all worked
together to create a holiday celebration that was simpler and
yet filled with fun and closeness.

Putting Others' Shoulds into Perspective
* Are you certain others really have those expectations?
* What information do you have that leads you to believe
  that?
* Check it out. Ask the people you have in mind whether
  they actually do expect you to be responsible for these
  tasks and activities.
* Or, ask them to join you in doing the exercises in Chapters Three and Four. Then you could share with each

other what is important and where the magic is. Perhaps, in this way, together you can plan and prepare for the kind of holiday that pleases you as a family.

* Let your imagination take you on a little trip. Pretend you are incapacitated during the holiday preparations. You have a terrible virus that lingers on. What would happen then? How important to others are the decorations? The feast? The gifts? If they had to do it themselves, what would they simplify or eliminate? Be aware of the expectations that others think are important only so long as you carry them out!

* Now imagine that you are partially ambulatory. You have recovered just enough to be present at the festivities. Your energy is still very limited, so you are attending this time strictly as a guest at events others have planned and worked on. Move these events in your mind's eye. What emotions do you experience? Are you enjoying yourself? Are you relieved? Or did they leave out of the celebration some facets that are important to you?

Perhaps now you have a clearer idea which activities are meaningful to others, which ones you care about, and also those to which nobody is terribly committed. You may have just become the owner of a JOB JAR that is no longer overwhelming! And you didn't have to get a virus in order to do it!

In your fantasy of attending holiday events as a guest, did you discover many aspects of the festivities are vital to *you?* Do you think the holiday is incomplete without including these items? Could it be that you do more of your tasks by choice than you thought? If that's true, why do they feel heavy for you?

Think about why you do this. For instance, be aware of how Mom or Dad acted at holiday time. Be aware of whether they approached the holiday preparations as if they were a lot of drudgery or something to be suffered over, complained about. Be aware of how you may be imitating their ways of coping or not coping with busy holiday schedules. Or, there may be a payoff for you in feeling overwhelmed — you feel important and needed. I know you can find ways of feeling important and needed that are more positive for you and for those around you.

Holiday tasks may have some elements of hard work, it's true. But I again propose to you that hard work and suffering don't necessarily go hand-in-hand. Dreading your chores long ahead of time is choosing to suffer. By doing so, you are trading being really alive in the present for existing miserably in your imagined future. And, strangely enough, suffering doesn't seem to help at all when it comes to actually accomplishing anything. Some alternatives to dreading your tasks or activities are:

  * Do the task efficiently and be done with it. Let it go.
  * Decide not to do it at all.
  * Plan a time when you will tackle that task, and think of how to reward yourself either before or after, or both! You could even put your rewards in your GIFT BOX, or write yourself an IOU, and put that in your GIFT BOX!
  * Do the task in a way or at a time when you can enjoy it.
  * Ask openly for the recognition or appreciation you want. Ask for strokes!
  * See that you are meeting your needs too. Go about your tasks as a self-full, rather than a selfless person.

As you reexamine your JOB JAR, you may feel locked into your usual ways of doing things. You may feel helpless, but it is not hopeless. You can reach into your store of creativity for several alternatives. It only seems that you are stuck because you've allowed yourself to get into a rut. We all do at times. I've heard it said the only difference between a rut and a grave is the depth of the excavation! I agree. Living more fully may be achieved by experimenting with new ways of going about holiday preparations.

The following real-life stories show how people found new

options. They took some steps to turn their OVERWHELM-ING JOB JARS into more joyful, manageable ones. Perhaps you will too.

Cecily used to send out two lists of Christmas cards, one of personal friends and one for Garson's business contacts. Garson was rarely motivated to make up his list until the last moment. Strangely enough, Cecily nagged him for years to give her his list, so that she might have the privilege of doing all that work! One time he was so late, they sent New Year's cards instead.

Two years ago Cecily tried a different approach and stated, "I'm willing to do your business cards before December nineteenth. After work on that day, I start wrapping gifts and decorating the house. This year I'm allowing enough time to have fun doing those projects, instead of rushing through them, and not really enjoying myself."

Garson did not submit his list, and no cards were sent to business acquaintances. Lo and behold! The earth didn't crumble! Garson's business continued to grow in spite of his failure to send greetings to customers and other VIPs. In fact, both he and they seemed blissfully unaware that something was missing.

Cecily found that an enlightening experience. One of her most startling discoveries was that she, far more than Garson, thought it was important for him to send cards to the business community. Cecily had been certain it was a method for paying his respects, keeping up his contacts, and making himself visible. She never did find out whether it actually served as an effective public relations technique, but she did know that failure to comply with this standard operating procedure was not harmful.

Since there were no disastrous effects, Cecily decided last year to also limit their personal Christmas card list. She continued to use season's greetings as a means of keeping in touch with out-of-town friends and acquaintances. This year she did not include most of the local folks. Instead, she made a point of personally extending her holiday wishes.

These are the ways in which Cecily pared down one of her least favorite Christmas chores and saved time and money as well. She used some of her extra money on dinner at a new fun restaurant the Saturday before Christmas. She thought that was a super idea, and so did Garson and the kids. For Cecily it was a double treat, because it allowed her to concentrate her culinary skills on Christmas baking instead of having to plan and cook dinner as well.

* * * * * *

Chad is a clergyman who thinks Christmas problems stem from a major conflict. On the one hand, we are reluctant to meet all the expectations and carry out all the traditions. On the other, we fear loneliness or disappointment.

His family used to frantically fit in visits to both sets of grandparents on Christmas Day. They even toted all the gifts along for the folks to see. Being rushed and then tired watered down their excitement. And the repeated feasting left them feeling lazy and stuffed. This last Christmas, illness prevented Chad and his family from carrying out this tradition. They found the quieter holiday much to their liking, as well as physically healthier and emotionally less stressful. Consequently, they have decided to spend Thanksgiving with one set of grandparents, and Christmas with the other, and to alternate each year. Chad is only regretful that he had to be sick in order to allow himself to deviate from tradition.

* * * * * *

Mara's most resented task was buying gifts for umpteen members of her family and her husband's. She spent days searching for the perfect gift, the most appropriate gift for each person. She even sought that unique, magic little item that would intrigue Great Aunt Tillie who had everything.

That required visiting little out-of-the-way shops and garrets and pouring over their stock or *objects d'art*.

Instead of complying with that routine, Mara made some changes this year. Since she is an artsy-craftsy person for whom holiday fun is synonymous with creative projects, she decided to start earlier, giving herself time to use her talents for making gifts for some of the relatives. As for the others, she decided to quickly pick items that were appealing to her and not to try to read the minds of the recipients. Of course, she was taking the risk that some people might not like the choices she made, but that had proven to be true even when Mara tried to find the perfect match between gift and recipient. So she decided to relax.

Mara succeeded in substituting happy and busy creativity for extensive shopping. She liked the holidays a whole lot better this year!

* * * * * *

Too many parties and too much drinking were what bothered Tess and George. They eliminated the party that they usually threw for friends and neighbors. They were afraid they would really miss what had become a tradition for them, but it must have been more of a hassle than a joy, because they didn't. They felt relieved. They spent the time they customarily would have used preparing for and hosting that party on the family activities they like. They built a snowman with the kids on one day. And on another they went trailing through the woods, playing and searching for a beautiful tree.

As for their office parties, Tess and George went later and left earlier. That felt better too. They also sharply curtailed their drinking and so eliminated those low-down hungover mornings. Much to Tess's delight, she had a rollicking good time when she didn't even have a sip of alcohol. She felt as witty as ever, maybe even more so.

* * * * * *

Greg usually staged an impressive production for his office staff. In actuality, it was his wife, Gretchen, who did all the planning and all the work, while Greg presided beneficiently over the finished product. Gretchen finally admitted to herself that she thoroughly hated the whole set-up, and she refused to repeat her previous performances. She was not willing to attend, to hostess, or to preside over the finished product for a change!

Greg, consequently, planned the party himself, and enlisted some help in the form of food trays provided by the local delicatessen. He did have to put more time and effort than usual into this endeavor, and he had some strong words with Gretchen about that. She responded by expressing her faith in him and encouraging Greg to create the party of his choice or to hire a caterer. Gretchen did not succumb to Greg's pressure. And she *almost* didn't feel guilty. She knew she had bent over backwards to please her husband for many years, and now she thought it was her turn. This time she was determined to please herself!

Greg did a fine job, and everyone let him know that. He wore a huge grin through most of his party and felt downright euphoric about his talent and resourcefulness. In fact, he soon exercised his newfound skills by throwing another party after a football game.

* * * * * *

Barbara made so many changes in her usual holiday practices that she made a list of them to celebrate with her friends.

* Instead of entertaining for family both Christmas Eve and Christmas Day, asked sister-in-law to be responsible for the first party.
* Not doing the whole dinner — asked everyone to bring something and the turkey was cooked by a local restaurant.
* Asked for gift suggestion lists from everyone.

55

* Took time off to go to concerts and plays.
* Asked for help with the cleaning.
* Accepted offers of help, such as with dishes and picking up after the meal.
* Didn't bother to bake cookies. We're all too fat.
* Had some fun doing the Christmassy things we really enjoy.

* * * * * *

As you read through the list of tasks in your JOB JAR, do you have the impression Christmas is a shared responsibility in your home? Your office? Which of the items on your list might you prefer to delegate to others? Take some time to think about that. Don't be too certain they can't or won't handle that responsibility.

For instance, Hannah loved shopping for gifts. Meandering down the noisy and crowded store aisles, exploring and choosing from the vast array of new and fascinating merchandise was a holiday activity she looked forward to all year long! But she hated wrapping her fantastic finds — it seemed like detail work to Hannah. And Hannah knew she was not a detail person.

Hannah relinquished the gift wrapping tasks to her daughter, Savannah. Savannah grumbled at times and did produce some packages that fell slightly short of Hannah's usual perfection. However, Savannah was feeling so important and so tickled with her rapidly growing skillfulness, that Hannah decided to share her appreciation rather than the additions or corrections she was tempted to make.

So relieved was Hannah that she then enlisted her husband, Sylvester, to wrap Savannah's gifts, and to make the decisions and purchases for the older nephews. Sylvester had been feeling left out of all the happy hubbub for years, and was delighted to be asked. In fact, he had wondered what was wrong with him. The holiday season had little impact on him. He felt pretty bah-humbug about it all. Sylvester experimented with taking on a few more responsibilities for his family's celebration. He was pleased to discover his increased investment of time, energy, and interest also increased his pleasure and feelings of being included.

* * * * * *

Henrietta's OVERWHELMING JOB JAR appeared in the beginning of this chapter. She decided to have a brainstorming session so she would have a whole bunch of alternatives from which to choose. The results of Henrietta's brainstorming session are included here. You, like Henrietta, can decide which of the alternatives you might use to make changes in your least favorite or least important items. You can also have a brainstorming session of your own.

As you reassess your JOB JAR and your priorities, perhaps some of these alternatives will be useful to you. I invite you to be your own Santa Claus by paring your JOB JAR down to a size that is no longer overwhelming for you. How many options can you brainstorm for dealing or not dealing with your low priority items?

Now go back to your WISHFUL JOB JAR. Since you are no longer the sole owner of an OVERWHELMING JOB JAR, perhaps you will now include some of the activities from your WISHFUL JOB JAR. I invite you to pay special attention to the events that have meaning or magic for you. You deserve a holiday full of your own special meaning and full of wishes *you* make come true. You deserve a holiday, a year, and a life you enjoy.

HAPPY HOLIDAYS!

A BRAINSTORMING SESSION
— on —
HENRIETTA'S OVERWHELMING JOB JAR

Task	Alternatives	Revised Time
Cards	* Pare down to out-of-town ones	4 hours
Out-of-town letters	* Duplicate basic letter and add personal notes	5 hours
Out-of-town gifts	* Buy quickly what appeals to me * Have stores or others do wrapping and mailing	1 day
Other gift shopping	* Have children buy their own gifts * Get suggestion lists from people * Use subscriptions and gift certificates	2 days
Select a tree	* Buy off Jaycee's lot	2 hours
Tree trimming party	* Ask everyone to bring a favorite food * Serve wine, cheese, and fruit * Have a big delicatessen tray	4 hours
Decorate house	* Turn it into a family project * Simplify decorations * Include in tree trimming party	2 hours
Clean house thoroughly	* Hire help * Ask Horace to vacuum * Ask relatives to help * Ask children to help * Do it less thoroughly — skip closets and cupboards	1 day
Horace's office party	* Go later, leave earlier	4 hours
My office party	* Bring contributions from deli or bakery	3 hours

Neighborhood party	* Skip it this year	-------
	* Make it pot luck	2 hours
	* Invite friends to cohost it	3 hours
	* Hire kitchen help	2 hours
Church party	* No change	4 hours
Family feast	* Ask family members to contribute food and help	1 day
	* Let someone else have it this year	-------
	* Buy turkey prepared and cooked	1 day
	* Hire kitchen help	1½ days
Housing out-of-town family	* Ask them to help prepare meals, or shop, or clean	
	* Don't offer steady entertainment	
	* Make only one or two meals per day	
	* Put them up in a local motel and we have a vacation too by joining them for swimming, eating out, and partying!	
Wrapping gifts	* Delegate to others	
	* Have stores do it	
Grocery shopping	* Have it delivered	1 hour
	* Send teenagers or other adults	
Get stocking fillers	* Each person over five buys for and fills at least one stocking	1 hour
Baking cookies	* Have a cookie-baking party	1 day
	* Make one kind and attend a cookie exchange	5 hours
	* Make fewer	1 day
	* Eliminate cookies	-------
	* Ask Mom or Mom-in-law to do it	-------

ADDED JOYS FROM MY GIFT BOX:

Church services	4 hours
Dinner out and special events with Horace	5 hours weekly
Attend presentations of *Nutcracker Suite* and Verdi's *Requiem*	1 afternoon 1 evening
Sew matching pajamas for all of us	2 days
Quiet time/relaxation	1/2 hour da

EIGHT

BEING SANTA CLAUS TO YOURSELF

Here is an outline of handy hints for gifts you can give yourself. They could be birthday, holiday, or year-round gifts. I hope you will repeatedly thumb through these pages and select from the items at any time you're looking for ways to be your own Santa Claus.

This chapter is a summary. Some of the hints appear here for the first time or are offered in a new way. Others have been mentioned earlier in the book and are important enough to bear repeating.

Handy Hints for Gifts to Give Yourself

1. *Determine what elements need to be present for the holiday to have meaning and magic for you.* Then take action. Find a way to build these factors into your holiday season. And give it your prime time and energy.

Don't get tired and harried with the mere trappings and end up with minimal time and energy for the things you really care about.

* If you are trying to create a spectacle or a production instead of a celebration, be aware of whom you're trying to impress or what motivates you. If you're doing it because you adore spectacles, hurray for you! If that is not the case, decide whether you are motivated strongly enough to be willing to carry the stress that may be involved.
* You probably won't be able to meet everyone else's standards or expectations for the holidays, so decide what your expectations are. You could compromise to some extent, but it would not be in your best interest to take on more than you can handle and juggle a whole bunch of expectations.

2. *Do very few things that you resent or strongly prefer not to do,* unless you are convinced it is worth the price that you

and others pay. Yes, others do pay a price for your selfless-ness or martyrdom. You may not consciously intend to exact a price, but you probably do in very subtle, or some not-so-subtle, ways. First of all, it can be mighty uncomfortable trying to relate to a "saint." Secondly, if you subjugate yourself to others' demands, you may expect them to march to your tune also.

For instance, let's imagine that I hate spending my precious Saturday shopping for my husband's gifts to business associ-ates, but I do it anyway. Well, I would certainly insist he take me out for dinner that night, in spite of the fact that he's been traveling and eating out all week and would prefer a sandwich at home. I could very well be thinking, "After all I've done for him! Don't I deserve some payoff for sacrificing my valuable time?" If I set it up to suffer enough, even his endless gratitude would be inadequate — I would still want more. I could end up irritable, short-tempered, and complain-ing.

3. If you need to, *allow others to be more responsible* for their own holiday celebration. Perhaps your brother Clyde thinks a tree is naked without popcorn strung around it. Perhaps Grandma thinks Christmas is incomplete unless the children are taken to the *Nutcracker Suite* and Dicken's *Christmas Carol*. Perhaps Dad thinks someone ought to travel 50 miles each way to go get Aunt Maude. Perhaps Aunt Maude thinks that minced pie is the only way to go. Let Clyde do it. Let Grandma do it. Let Dad do it. And let Aunt Maude do it. You don't have to do it all for them. If people really want something, they will be willing to contribute some effort to make it happen.

People, even younger ones, can be responsible for the gifts they choose. You don't have to do that for them either. Johnny's present for his teacher may be somewhat inappro-priate in your opinion, but she knows Johnny well and will probably chuckle over it. Janie can pick her best friend's gift, and Clyde his secretary's. And if Mom says she doesn't know what Clyde likes, she can always give him a gift certificate. You can't shop for everybody, and there are limits to your ingenuity and resourcefulness. You could arrange a swap. For example, if Mom knows better what to get for your sister Joanne, she could take care of that for you, while you take care of Clyde's for her.

4. *Acknowledge and feel your feelings.* Feelings need not be justified or logical. It is unrealistic and restricting to allow oneself only certain emotions, such as joy and good will. Negative feelings may not be pleasant, but they are part of life. To allow yourself to feel all your feelings is to be fully alive.

5. *Let others feel their feelings too.* They, also, can be expected to have some unholiday-like emotions. You are not responsible for their feelings. *They* are. You do not have to "fix" their feelings. It is not healthy for you to try to direct others out of one feeling and into a different one. It is not healthy for people to be allowed only the "right" feelings.

6. *Live in the here and now.* Breathe deeply. Feel yourself breathe. Feel your body move. Use your senses. Notice what you see, what you hear, what you smell. You *will* need to make some decisions and some plans for the forthcoming holiday. And looking forward to it can be enjoyable. But don't give up your present for the future. Don't give up your November for December. November is one-twelfth of the year, and you deserve to live and cherish each month and each day.

7. For some people, feeling their emotions and staying in the present could involve grieving. If you're missing some people or elements that were present at previous holidays, *you may need to mourn* them. Grief is not limited to traumatic events like the death of a parent or spouse. Mourning is an everyday process that needs to occur whenever changes take place.

You may be recently divorced. Your children or friends may have moved away. You may miss your old neighbors or perhaps you have a new job, a new house. Allowing yourself to mourn some of those changes or losses will, not right now,

but in the long run, enable you to more easily let go of the
past and stay in the present.

Mary and Jay did that for themselves the first year they
celebrated without the children. They acknowledged their
need for some new ideas for their changed lifestyle. They
recognized their feelings and allowed themselves to do some
mourning for the old raucous family gatherings. They did
give a party for their church group. That lent a more festive
feeling to their holiday.

* * * * * *

Susan had some letting go to do too. Each of the last ten
years she and the kids, Peter and Bonnie, had spent several
days creating and concocting marvelous new varieties and
huge quantities of cookies. One year they made one thousand
of them!

Last year, it was a real battle to find a time when everyone
was available for the task. Susan did most of the work herself, and it was no fun that way. She thought, "Poor me."
This year, Bonnie and Peter both had part-time jobs and a
packed social schedule as well. They said they loved and
wanted all those cookies, especially the gingerbread people,
but it was obvious they didn't want them badly enough to do
anything about it. Jobs were top priority, then friends and
social life, then skiing, then sleeping in. It seemed as if
cookies were important only if Mom did them.

Susan had enough of martyrdom last year! She bid a
reluctant farewell to the good old fun-filled days of having
cookies in various stages of preparation covering every available surface in the kitchen and dining room. Instead, she
made one large batch by herself and took them to a cookie
exchange. She had fun partying with the other women and
began a friendship with a new neighbor. She came home with
a lovely assortment of cookies, feeling content.

8. It is time to *let go of past disappointments* too. If your
past few holidays, or those of your childhood were dreadful,

let go of that past. You can take the necessary steps to make this holiday what you want it to be or you can set it up so that this one is dreadful too. And then you can say to yourself or others, "See, I told you holidays are perfectly awful." If you need some professional help to get out of that self-defeating rut, find it, and use it.

9. *Ask for what you want.* You may think it's clearly evident that you need help with certain tasks, or compliments for having successfully completed others. It may not be that obvious to other people. They have a different frame of reference. They see it through different eyes. They have different thoughts running through their minds.

* Ask for the help you want. You have every right to make your needs known. Don't hint. Don't complain about how much you have to handle. Simply communicate straight. Ask such questions as:
  * Will you take care of selecting the tree this year?
  * The packages have to be mailed Tuesday. Will you help me wrap them before then?
  * I know I usually shop for all the gifts, even though they're from both of us. I need you to pick out Uncle Ned's and your brother Clyde's this year.
  * It is important to me that our party be a shared task this year. When are you willing to sit down with me to decide who does what as far as preparations are concerned?

* Ask for the gifts you want. Again, don't hint. Write a list and share it with family members, or tack a note on the refrigerator door. If you have no specific desires, or you prefer surprises, then skip this one. But if there is something you especially want, don't hint or be vague. Don't put yourself in the position of waiting and hoping for Santa Claus at Christmas and Prince Charming or Lady Luck all year around. Make it happen! If you are the only one you can depend on, give yourself that gift. (See number eleven).

* Ask for the strokes you want. Some examples:
  • Didn't I do a beautiful job on the tree?
  • I put a lot of time and thought into making your gifts, and I want you to tell me how creative I am.
  • I need my back rubbed. Will you do that?
  • I need taking care of right now. Is it okay if I put my head in your lap?
  • You could also ask for written strokes — little one-liners saying what people like about you or what you are doing. Some of your resources might be children, family, friends, neighbors, and co-workers.

10. *Take good care of yourself.*
  * Nourish yourself with the kinds and quantity of food and drink that are healthy for you. If you gorge on rich foods, junk foods, or sweets, or imbibe too much alcohol, you will pay the price in reduced physical and emotional well-being. After the initial reaction, both sugar and alcohol have an eventual negative effect on your mood, your energy level, and your physical health. Gifting yourself with a weight gain or a hangover is no way to be your own Santa Claus!
  * Be sure you get enough sleep. There are bound to be occasions when sleep is the last thing you're interested in. But do allow yourself makeup time, and don't neglect your sleep needs on a regular basis. If you exhaust yourself or feel tense or irritable, you may ruin your holiday fun.
  * Put aside some time for rest or relaxation every day. Do whatever feels good for you or what works for you during your time. You could catch a catnap, gaze at the clouds, daydream, take a bubble bath or a long shower. You could buy yourself a relaxation tape, the book *The Relaxation Response,* or a course in transcendental meditation.
  * Allow yourself to have the withdrawal time you need. If you have house guests, or are at a family gathering and

need some quiet time, take it. You could take a nap or a walk, doodle, or make a telephone call. Yoga, calisthenics, or some other form of physical exercise might feel good. The authors of *The Book of Hope* point out how impossible it is to remain depressed while engaged in physical activity. You are entitled to take whatever time you need for withdrawal and physical activity.

* Do at least one thing each day simply because you want to, or because you feel like it. Have some fun!

11. Be a self-full person: *Fill your bucket yourself.* You are a valuable human being. You deserve strokes. You deserve some of life's goodies. Whether or not you have people in your life who also provide for some of your needs or wants, you will need to learn to act in your own behalf. No matter how many loving folks you know, they may be unavailable to meet your needs. In the final analysis, the person you can depend on is you! Saying what you need, asking for what you want is one way. (See number nine.) In case that doesn't work, you can do some of that for yourself.

* You can give yourself strokes quietly and internally. You can do that by noticing more details about how well you are handling your tasks or your life, or what a neat person you are, instead of taking all that for granted. Some examples:
  • I did that much more efficiently than last time.
  • I really kept my cool during that crisis.
  • Imagine! I handled several issues simultaneously and didn't get confused.
  • I am a neat person and getting neater every day.
  • I only procrastinated half as long as usual.
  • I deserve to be important.
  • I was only depressed about X's criticism for one hour this time. I bet I can soon get it down to twenty minutes!
  • What a creative person I am.
  • I am a smart woman/man.

When you want to improve, to grow, you may choose to notice your shortcomings and criticize yourself for them. Everybody makes mistakes, and you can learn from yours. However, criticism or negative strokes alone are not effective motivators for many people. What works for most folks is the addition of positive strokes too. They need to notice and appreciate their gains, their successes. The combination that I favor is two positives for every negative. Write down some of your neatest strokes to yourself, and add them to your GIFT BOX.

* You could also say your strokes to yourself out loud, and perhaps others would accept your invitation and give you strokes too. In any event, it is likely to have a positive effect on your self-esteem. For instance:
  * I sure did a good job on those decorations.
  * Look at those cookies. What a work of art!
  * I'm getting more and more inventive with my wrappings.
  * I was very efficient about arranging to have the car fixed.
  * I did a marvelous job on this meal.
  * I'm a warm, caring person.
  * I'm so thoughtful to serve you breakfast in bed.
* Give yourself some tangible gifts too. You are worth it. Spending money on other folks is generous and thoughtful. You count too. Be generous and thoughtful with yourself also.
* Start with any:
  * books
  * tapes
  * classes that will help you with your relaxation time
* You could add
  * other books
  * classes of a personal growth or spiritual nature that will help sustain you or give you a lift during this season and on through the year
  * posters

- poetry
- a book of quotations

* Buy yourself a treat. Don't overextend yourself financially gifting others so that you have nothing left for treats to yourself.
  - tickets to events that you enjoy
  - going to a special place for dinner
  - a massage
  - hairdo
  - shave
  - manicure
  - Make a list of items that feel like treats to you, and choose one when your morale needs a boost or because you want to.
* Purchase at least a few little appealing objects for yourself.
  - If the gift you've bought for Cousin Ted means so much to you that you hate to give it away, how about getting one for you too?
  - Or grab that coffee mug that strikes your fancy.
  - If you need a nice, warm pair of boots, why not right now?
  - If toy shopping sets you yearning, give in to that yearning. Big people deserve toys too. They even deserve little kids' toys. I just bought myself a big, brand-new teddy bear.
* Perhaps the most important investment you could make for yourself would be hiring or paying for whatever kind of help you need for the holiday season.
  - For a small fee, department stores will wrap and mail your packages.
  - Many stores even have a shopping service.
  - You can have a party catered.
  - Hire kitchen help.
  - Buy some foods already prepared by restaurants or supermarkets that render that service.

- For just a few dollars, you can have your groceries delivered.
* It's a good time of year to be employing youngsters. Many of them are eager to earn money, and could be of assistance with:
  - baby-sitting
  - snow-shoveling
  - errand-running
  - housecleaning
  - other chores

Think what kind of help would make it a better holiday for you. Add these decisions to the growing pile of goodies in your GIFT BOX.

* If you can afford it, plan a larger purchase for yourself too.
  - If you buy clothing for family members while you're wishing to spruce up your own wardrobe, you could indulge yourself.
  - If you have an out-of-town friend whom you don't have time to drive up to see, how about an airline ticket?
  - A long-distance call.

Write down your decisions and put them in the GIFT BOX you created for yourself, or include the bills, your reaction to the event, or the merchandise itself.

* To accomplish things, give yourself
  - the permission,
  - the determination, and
  - the courage.

The mere idea of doing something new can be fun and stimulating. (See the appendix for gift hints.)

* Learn to receive at least as gracefully as you give. I think that is a beautiful talent that threatens to fall into disuse. As an important person, you deserve to receive as well as give goodies. Not only that, other people are as entitled

to experience the joys of giving and feeling needed as you are.

I think it would be splendid for all if the mechanics and the meaning of the holidays could be a shared experience — the doing for others and the having things done for you, the giving and the receiving, the planning and the carrying out of plans, the cherishing of some old traditions and the discarding of others.

Most of all, I invite you to act on your needs. If you need to, evolve new ways of celebrating — ways that combine the best parts of tradition with new activities that reflect you and your lifestyle. I urge you to think about, plan, prepare for, and celebrate a season that is fitting for you, that will work for you, and that meets your needs.

Have a good holiday!

Have a good life!

APPENDIX

MORE THOUGHTS ON GIFTING

Hints for Giving and Receiving

1. Do not let the media or the merchants orchestrate your holiday.
2. Avoid competing in size of gifts, trees, parties, quantity of food or drink, and amount of financial disaster.
3. Once again, setting your own standards is the key. If materialism or limited finances bother you, choose where you would like to place your emphasis.
   * Maybe you prefer to give of yourself, your time, your effort. The following are some ideas for inexpensive gifts to be both given and requested.
     - IOUs for specific chores
     - IOUs for physical or verbal strokes
     - invitation to a meal at your home
     - invitation to a meal out
     - a private concert by the musically talented
     - typing services
     - IOU for a gripe-free day
     - a sample of a person's unique creativity, such as: art, furniture, food, clothing, poetry, handiwork
     - companionship for a special event or a special day
     - transportation to the above
     - offering a specific time to be together on a regular basis
   * There are also some other ways of approaching gift giving and getting that are less demanding of time, money, or ingenuity. Almost all could be annual gifts if they met the recipient's needs.
     - stationery and postage stamps
     - subscriptions to professional journals or special interest magazines
     - cheese trays
     - fruit baskets

* Shut-ins or those who hate to shop could use all of the above, plus:
  * groceries, including canned fish and meat, and packaged products that don't spoil
  * a box of greeting cards
  * a newspaper subscription
* Family gifts (A purchase or idea that is desirable to a number of people in the family and that takes the place of some of the individual gifts.) EXAMPLE: One year the total gift exchange in the Smith family consisted of a ping pong table, an extension telephone, and dinner out followed by tickets to a special concert. These were items that all four family members wanted and enjoyed. The decision evolved out of necessity. The total amount of time, effort, and money spent on gifts had been steadily increasing. And, strangely enough, so had the number of disappointments. Each person had very specific ideas about clothing, records, books, and other possibilities. It almost seemed as if they didn't want others to make any selections for them, so they brainstormed a happy alternative.
* To save yourself a lot of time and sore feet, use catalog and telephone orders if it pleases you.
* If infinite and intense shopping is not to your liking, pick out what appeals to you quickly and spontaneously. Frequently one's first impulse is the best anyway!

A CHRISTMAS LETTER

If you like to send holiday letters, this one may give you some ideas. I encourage you to share *yourself* in your letters — not just your successes, possessions, and travels. Include both the positive and negative aspects of your feelings, experiences, and opinions.

Dear Friends,

Janie is taking driver's training now and shows every indication of becoming an excellent driver. Apparently, our car is safe. In fact, we're somewhat chagrined by the possibility that it might be safer in Janie's hands than in ours. While we don't feel exactly elated when she points out the ways in which our driving skills have deteriorated, we're lucky to have a resident expert at our house. We're shaping up nicely, thank you! Now there are two fewer slipshod drivers on the road.

This year for Johnny's eleventh birthday, we all spent a couple of days tracking down his dream bike. Bikes sure are complicated now. Have you ever heard of side-pull caliper handbrakes; a twist-grip gear shifter; an extended front fork; touring, motocross-style, or high-rise handlebars; a wide, touring, or banana-style saddle? No? Well we hadn't either! And it wasn't easy to decide what features were best. But Johnny was ecstatic over the bike we selected together.

Johnny and his friend Tom have been ranging far and wide on their bikes. And that was a problem for us for a while. John resented our restrictions on the places and distances he could go, and we were apprehensive about the grandiose plans he and Tommy were making. After much hassling, we've reached a compromise. The boys have joined a bike club which they enjoy and which offers the supervision we think is still necessary.

The school is having some unusual effects on our lives this year. Each of the children has one teacher who presents the subject in such enticing ways that the kids are eager and curious. Both John and Jane are thinking and researching beyond the class requirements. They are sharing their findings with us, and we are changing some of the ways we live.

John is delving into nutrition and diet. He uses a marvelous recipe his teacher gave him to make granola for us from fresh grains, dried fruits, and honey purchased at the co-op. Wow — and have we learned about the ill effects of sugar. We eat differently and buy differently now. And we feel gr-r-r-eat!

Jane is studying about the ecological balance. Or maybe I should say we all are. We've changed some of the soap products we use and are back to wrapping the garbage instead of using the disposal.

We're so proud of our kids! They're thinking, caring people. They care about their bodies and their environment.

Samantha reluctantly took the promotion to account executive at the ad agency. She was really hard on herself at first. She expected, and thought others expected, that she would emerge on day one as a proficient, experienced success story! Her fear that she wouldn't meet those standards almost caused her to back off from the opportunity. She was plenty scared but dove in anyway. She's currently plugging away, learning the ropes, doing beautifully at times and poorly at others, just like the old hands!

Being self-employed is just what the doctor ordered for Chuck! It was an unnerving, precarious existence for a while. In the long haul, though, he thrives on the simpler, less pressured lifestyle, and likes not having anyone to second-guess his decisions. And he doesn't miss all those long, tense meetings.

We went camping 300 miles north to the "wilderness." Some wilderness! Johnny bruised his knee stumbling around in the undergrowth of beverage cans! We now have a family joke about "roughing it"! Seriously though, sitting in a boat in the middle of a vast expanse of water was heavenly. When our experience consisted of only the wind and water, the sun and sky and each other, our lives seemed to fall into place.

We came home refreshed, replenished, and with a new perspective.

We all wish you a delightful holiday season and a year of good health, love, and laughter.

The Swensons

JOB JAR WORKSHEET

_____
_____
_____
_____
_____
_____
_____
_____
_____
_____
_____
_____
_____
_____
_____
_____
_____
_____
_____
_____
_____

WISHFUL JOB JAR WORKSHEET

_____

_____

_____

_____

_____

_____

_____

_____

_____

_____

_____

_____

_____

_____

_____

_____

_____

_____

_____

_____

_____

SUGGESTED READINGS

Bach, George and Goldberg, Herb, *Creative Aggression: The Art of Assertive Listening,* New York, Avon Books, 1975.

Benson, Herbert and Klipper, Miriam Z., *The Relaxation Response,* New York, Avon Books, 1976.

Clark, Jean Illsley, *Self-Esteem: A Family Affair,* Minneapolis, Winston Press, 1981.

Colgrove, Melba, Bloomfield, Harold H., and McWilliams, Peter, *How to Survive the Loss of a Love,* New York, Bantam Books, 1977. Available through Hazelden Educational Materials, order no. 6452.

DeRosis, Helen A. and Pellegrino, Victoria Y., *The Book of Hope: How Women Can Overcome Depression,* New York, Bantam Books, 1977.

James, Muriel and Jongeward, Dorothy, *Born to Win,* New York, National American Library, 1978.

Kopp, Sheldon B., *If You Meet the Buddha on the Road, Kill Him!,* New York, Bantam Books, 1976. Available through Hazelden Educational Materials, order no. 6474.

O'Neill, Nena and O'Neill, George, *Shifting Gears,* New York, Avon Books, 1975.

Smith, Manuel J., *When I Say No, I Feel Guilty,* New York, Bantam Books, 1975. Available through Hazelden Educational Materials, order no. 6655.

Hazelden

Other titles that will interest you...

Today's Gift

Today's Gift is our first daily meditation book written with the family in mind. A collection of readings written specifically to help us, as individuals, deal with our family concerns. *Today's Gift* is an excellent companion for those of us involved in A.A., Al-Anon, Alateen, Adult Children of Alcoholics, and other self-help groups. *Today's Gift* will inspire discussion among family members — child and adult alike — and help us all to pause, regain a sense of balance, and recognize the riches we have within and around us. (400 pp.)
Order No. 1031A

The Love Book
by Karen Casey

From one of the authors of *The Promise of a New Day*, a collection of weekly meditations exploring the topic of love. In each of the fully-illustrated 52 meditations, Karen Casey sensitively examines the challenge of love: the love we show friends, family, ourselves, a lover, or even a stranger. *The Love Book* is a celebration of life for all of us who have struggled to learn to express, and to accept, love. *The Love Book* reaffirms our search for a simple joy in being — believing that we are loveable, and learning to risk love and care, without fear. (110 pp.)
Order No. 5050A

For price and order information, please call one of our Customer Service Representatives.

Hazelden
Educational Materials

Pleasant Valley Road
Box 176
Center City, MN 55012-0176

(800) 328-9000
(Toll Free. U.S. Only.)
(800) 328-0500
(Toll Free. Film and Video Orders. U.S. Only.)
464-8844
(Toll Free. Metro Twin Cities.)
(612) 257-4010
(MN, AK, & Outside U.S.)